ANCIENT GREECE

Contents

Introduction

This is a map of Greece. Today, thousands of people visit Greece each year to enjoy the hot summer sunshine and swim in the warm blue sea. Many visit Athens, which is the biggest city in Greece.

Try and find Greece in an atlas.

▼ **Athens and the Acropolis today.**

Today Athens is a big modern city. In the middle of Athens stands a big hill called the <u>Acropolis</u>. On the Acropolis are some wonderful buildings. They were built more than 2,000 years ago by the Ancient Greeks.

LOOKING AT EVIDENCE

The buildings on the Acropolis give us clues about how the Ancient Greeks lived. These things help us to find out more.

▶ Statue of the Greek goddess Athene.

▲ This is the golden mask of a Greek king which was found in his grave.

A	B	G	D	E	Z/SD
E	Th	I	K	L	M
N	X/Ks		O	P	R	S
T	U	Ph/F		Kh/Ch	Ps	O

▲ These are Ancient Greek letters. The nearest letters in English are written beneath them. The Ancient Greeks wrote many books.

The Greeks at sea

Much of mainland Greece is very mountainous. The rocky hills made travelling by land difficult for the Ancient Greeks. There was very little flat land for sowing crops. Two crops that grew well were grapevines and olive trees.

Many Greeks built ships to travel by sea to make new homes for themselves in other countries or to trade. They became great seafarers travelling long distances. Sometimes they came home very rich.

Stone anchor with wooden stakes.

The helmsman steered the ship with two rudders.

Greek merchant ships had a large square sail on a single mast. If the weather turned bad Greek sailors would try to reach a port or beach their ship on land to avoid the storm.

The best time to go sailing is July or August. You won't wreck your ship or drown your sailors then. In high summer the sea is usually calm and the winds are gentle. Do your best to set sail then, but make sure you come back before autumn. Then the fierce North wind makes the sea dangerous.

Why did the Greeks need to trade?

1 We Greeks make good pottery and have plenty of wine and olive oil. But we don't grow enough grain to eat. I am going to sail to Egypt to trade.

2 I swap my wine, olive oil and pottery for grain, gems, ivory, and papyrus.

3 Now I can sell these things in Athens. I hope I don't meet any pirates on the way.

Some sailors painted an eye on the bow to keep away evil spirits or help guide the ship on its way.

▼ The painting on this vase shows a merchant ship being attacked by a pirate ship.

Most of the cargo is kept below deck.

◄ Hesiod is one of the earliest Greek writers whose books we know about. Hesiod wrote this advice to sailors in Ancient Greek.

The cities

Ancient Greece was not ruled over by one person. Different parts of the country were ruled by different cities. The two strongest cities were Athens and Sparta.

Sparta was ruled by two kings. These kings told the people what to do.

The Athenians did not have kings. They had a democracy. They held big meetings on a hill called the Pnyx. Here the people decided how their city should be run.

Women and slaves were not allowed to go to the Pnyx to speak and vote.

Mount Olympus

Delphi

Olympia

Mediterranean Sea

Epid

Sparta

▼ Athens had a democracy.

▼ Sparta was ruled by two kings.

Aegean Sea

Troy

Marathon

thens
mis

CRETE

▲ **Pericles.**

Pericles was a famous Athenian who helped to start the democracy. In Ancient Greece he wrote:

Our kind of government is different from that of our neighbors. Our kind of government is called democracy. This means that power is in the hands of the people as a whole, not just a chosen few.

Athens

On the hill in Athens called the Acropolis we can still see the remains of temples which were built from marble. The people of Ancient Athens built these temples for their gods and goddesses. They also used the Acropolis as a fortress in times of war.

The Parthenon is the biggest of the temples. It was built for Athene, the goddess of Athens.

At the bottom of the Acropolis were houses, other temples, and the market place called the agora.

The columns around the temple called the Erechtheum were statues of women.

Sacred olive tree.

Huge bronze statue of Athene. On clear days it could be seen by sailors out at sea.

◄ The Erechtheum is a temple on the Acropolis. This is what it looks like today.

The Parthenon had huge marble columns and a wooden roof covered in tiles. All around the roof were stone carvings and statues.

Athenians brought animals to the altar for priests to <u>sacrifice</u>.

▲ The Acropolis has been attacked many times and much of it has been destroyed, but the marble ruins that still remain show us how wonderful it must have looked.

9

The Parthenon

The Parthenon is one of the most famous buildings in the world. In ancient times the marble statues and sculptures around its roof would have been painted in bright colors. They told the stories of gods and heroes. This sculpture shows a fighting centaur.

How was the Parthenon built?

1. ▲ White marble was cut from a mountain about 10 miles from Athens. The marble was cut into blocks to make the temple walls, and into drums to make the columns.

2. ▼ This marble was carried by carts pulled by oxen to the foot of the Acropolis, and then checked to make sure it had no cracks or faults.

4. ◄ Stone-masons used iron and bronze tools to shape the blocks and drums. They lifted the marble with pulleys and cranes, and moved it into place with levers. H-shaped iron clamps were used to hold the blocks of marble together.

3. ▲ Mules dragged the marble up the hill. The mules that worked the hardest were allowed to go free as a reward.

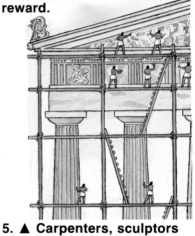

5. ▲ Carpenters, sculptors and artists finished the temple roof and decorations.

Inside the Parthenon

A giant statue of Athene, over 32 feet tall, stood inside the Parthenon. The statue's face, arms and feet were covered in white ivory and her clothes were covered with plates of gold. Her eyes were made of precious stones.

At the foot of the statue was a pool of water. This kept the room cool and stopped the ivory from cracking in the summer heat.

This is what the inside of the Parthenon may have looked like. The gold and ivory statue of Athene held a figure of Nike, the goddess of victory, in one hand.

Markets and shops

In the middle of every city was the market place or agora. It was a busy place full of market stalls and workshops. People went to the agora to buy food, clothes, and other goods. It was also a place where they could meet their friends and have a chat.

Around the agora were the banks, law courts and town hall.

Long colonnades called stoa surrounded the agora.

People often met friends and chatted in the cool shade under the colonnades.

There was often a statue of a famous person in the agora.

◀ These women are collecting water from a fountain. The pots which are held upright are filled with water, the pots on their sides are empty.

▲ Bottom of a vase showing a picture of a shoemaker.

Traders set up their stalls in the middle of the agora.

13

War with Persia

Next to Ancient Greece was a powerful country called Persia. The king of Persia was called Darius. The Persians had a strong army with many skillful <u>archers</u>. Darius used his army to attack and invade other countries. Soon he had built a great <u>empire</u> that was so big it took 90 days on horseback to cross it to reach the capital city, Persepolis.

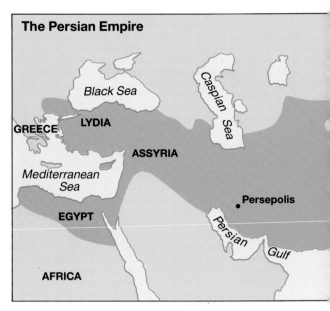

The Persian Empire

GREECE

Black Sea

Caspian Sea

LYDIA

ASSYRIA

Mediterranean Sea

Persepolis

EGYPT

Persian Gulf

AFRICA

The Marathon runner

2. Pheidippides had to run all the way back to Marathon with the bad news.

1. The Greek runner called Pheidippides had to run all the way to Sparta to ask for help. But the Spartans were celebrating a religious <u>festival</u> and would not come until the next full moon.

3. After helping to defeat the Persians, Pheidippides was told to run to Athens and tell the people about the victory. He ran all the way but died of exhaustion after delivering his news.

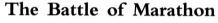

The Battle of Marathon

Darius decided to invade Greece. He sent a huge army and navy to attack the Athenians. The Persians landed at the Bay of Marathon. The Athenians sent a runner called Pheidippides to Sparta to ask for help, but the Spartans arrived too late to help. The Persian army was much larger than the Athenian army. But by clever <u>tactics</u> the Athenian <u>hoplite</u> soldiers defeated the Persians.

The Greek historian Herodotus tells us that the Persians lost 6,400 men, but the Athenians lost only 192.

Warships

After Darius died, Xerxes became king of the Persians. He decided to get his revenge and marched into Greece with a huge army. He also brought more than a thousand ships with him. Xerxes' men tied ships together to make bridges across the sea which separates Asia from Europe.

The Battle of Salamis

In 480 BC the Greek triremes attacked the Persian navy between the island of Salamis and the mainland. The large Persian ships were difficult to steer in these narrow waters. The smaller triremes rammed and sank most of the Persian navy. The Persians never tried to invade Greece again.

When a great storm destroyed the bridges, Xerxes told us to give the sea 300 lashes with a whip.

Triremes

The Athenians built 200 special warships called triremes. Triremes were very powerful, with three rows of oarsmen on each side. A ram was fixed to the front end of the ship. The ram was used to make a hole in the side of enemy ships.

Triremes were about 135 feet long and 20 feet wide. The oars were about 13 feet long.

The linen sail was used when the trireme was in open sea.

Soldiers travelled on the ship's deck.

Three rows of oarsmen.

The two oars at the back were used to steer the ship.

Bronze ram, used to sink enemy ships.

▲ The picture on this vase shows a Greek warship.

17

Sparta

Sparta, like Athens, is one of the best known cities of Ancient Greece. But <u>archaeologists</u> have found little evidence of wonderful Spartan buildings or great artists or thinkers. Sparta is famous for its well-trained and powerful army.

The city of Sparta started as several villages. The Spartans defeated their neighbors in wars and turned them into slaves. The Spartans feared that one day they might be attacked by other enemy cities or by their slaves. They decided to build a mighty army by training their children from a young age to be soldiers.

Life for a Spartan child.

Every newborn baby was shown to the Spartan city elders. If it looked weak it had to be taken to the mountains and left to die.

At the age of seven, boys were taken away from their parents and trained to become soldiers. They had to march without any shoes, their hair was shaved off, and they had only a cloak to keep them warm in winter.

Sparta and Athens at war.

In 431 B.C. Athens and Sparta quarrelled and went to war. Other cities soon joined in what is called the <u>Peloponnesian War</u>. The Athenians feared the powerful Spartan army and so they built great walls around their city. After many years the Spartans defeated the Athenians, but both sides were weakened by the terrible war.

They have to steal what they get.
If anyone is caught, he is given several lashes with a whip.

▲ This is what one Greek writer wrote about Spartan boys.

During their training Spartan boys were given very poor food. They were told that it was not wrong to steal food, as long as they were clever enough not to get caught.

Spartan girls were also made to exercise so that they would have strong babies when they grew up. They had to run, wrestle, and throw the javelin and the discus.

▲ Bronze statue of a Spartan girl running.

19

Everyday life in Ancient Greece

Life for women

Life in Ancient Greece was different for rich and poor, and for men and women.

▲ **This picture on a Greek pot shows a woman spinning.**

In Athens, only girls from rich families had lessons. They learned to read and write. They also learned music and arithmetic. They were given lessons so that they would become good housewives. They often married when they were only 14 years old.

Rich women took charge of the slaves in their household. The women made sure that the children were looked after, that meals were cooked, and spent a lot of time weaving and spinning cloth. They were not allowed to go out of the house very often.

Poorer women had to work hard, with no slaves to help them, but they had more freedom to go where they wanted.

Life for men

Rich Athenian boys usually spent much longer at school than girls. They learned to write as well as to read. They also had music lessons and had plenty of physical education. Poorer families could not afford to send their sons to school for long.

At the age of 18 young men had to fight in the army for two years. Sometimes they went on to further education where they learned subjects like mathematics, science and geography.

Men often did the same jobs as their fathers. Some worked as farmers or as fishermen. Others went to sea as sailors or as oarsmen in the triremes.

▲ Babies were sometimes looked after by a nurse. This vase painting shows a nurse handing a baby to its mother.

▼ The painting on this vase shows a Greek boy having a music lesson. The boy is playing pipes and his teacher is playing the lyre.

Look at page 18 to find out what life was like for a Spartan child.

An Ancient Greek house

This picture shows what the house of a rich Greek may have looked like inside. In the middle of the house is an open courtyard, but the only way into the house is through an entrance door which could be locked.

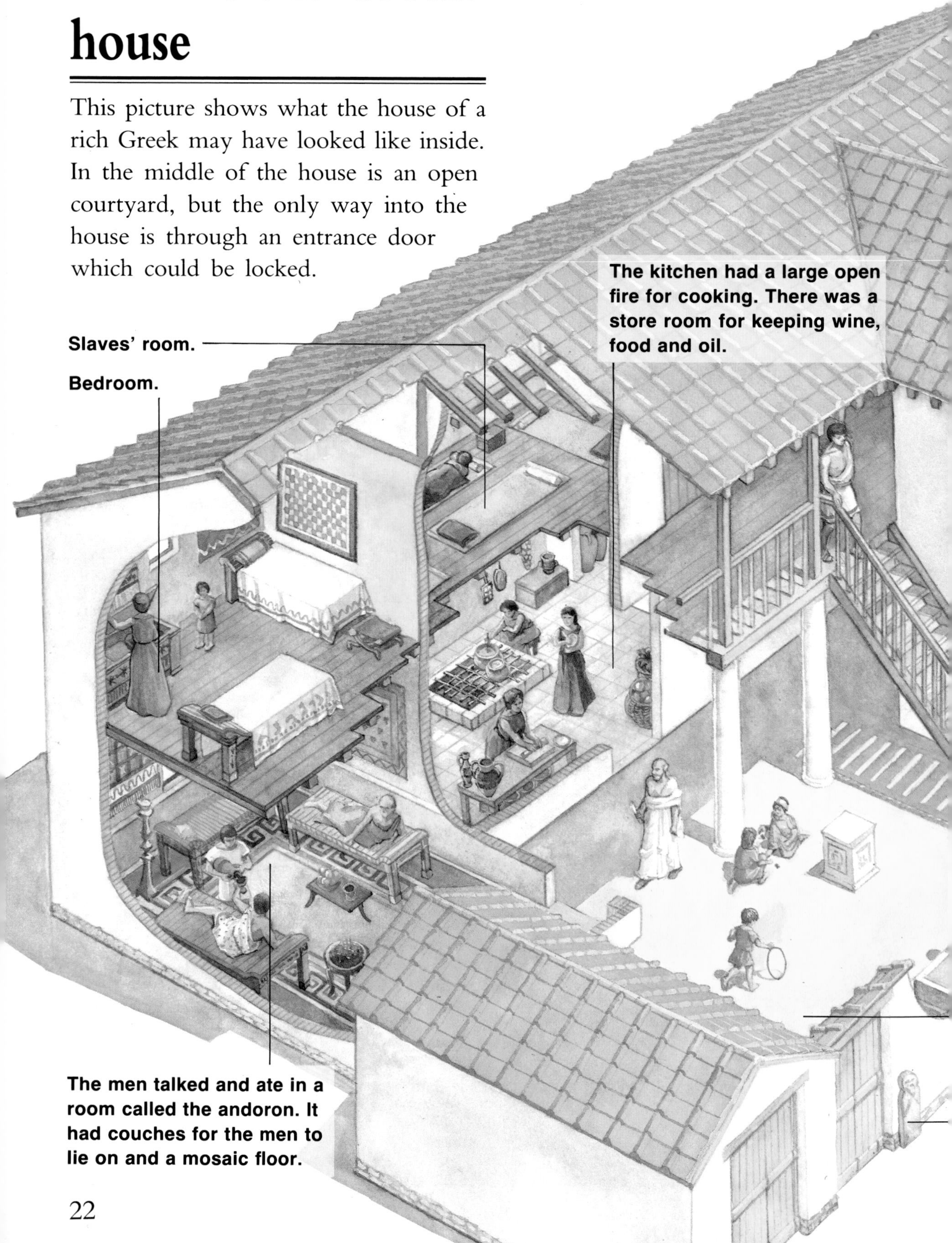

The kitchen had a large open fire for cooking. There was a store room for keeping wine, food and oil.

Slaves' room.

Bedroom.

The men talked and ate in a room called the andoron. It had couches for the men to lie on and a mosaic floor.

The house was built from mud bricks, with a clay tiled roof.

The women talked to their friends, organized the household, and did spinning and weaving in a room called the gynaeceum.

LOOKING AT EVIDENCE

▼ Pottery baby's feeding bottle. The writing says in Greek "Drink, don't stop!"

▼ Sculpture of children playing a Greek game called Knucklebones.

The bathroom had a terra cotta washstand and bath.

In the courtyard there was an altar where prayers were said, and a well to provide water.

Many people had a statue of the god Hermes outside their front door to keep evil away.

Ancient Greeks at work

Working on the land

Many people lived in the countryside around Athens. They worked as farmers and grew grain, grapes, figs and other fruit. They also grew olive trees. Oil from the olives was used for cooking, and in oil lamps for lighting. Some farmers kept pigs, sheep, goats and beehives to make honey.

▼ **Some Ancient Greeks went hunting for their food.**

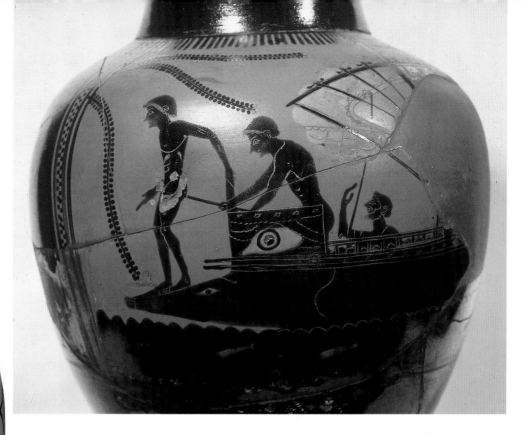

▲ The painting on this vase shows Greek fishermen at work.

◄ The painting on this vase shows an olive harvest. The men beat the tree with sticks so the olives fall to ground, then they are collected in a basket.

▲ A silver coin from Athens. The owl was a sign of the goddess Athene.

Working on the sea

Many Ancient Greeks earned their living on the water. Some were fishermen, some were traders. Many Athenian men worked as oarsmen on the triremes.

Slaves

There were large numbers of slaves in Ancient Greece, owned by people in the same way that we own pets today. They were often people the Greeks had captured during wars.

Some slaves were owned by families, working in the family home or on the farm. Many had to work in the Athenian silver mines. Silver from the mines was used to make Athenian coins. Working in these mines was dirty and very dangerous.

The potter at work

There was no plastic in ancient times. The Ancient Greeks used pottery to make things like bottles, jars and bowls.

There were many potters who worked in Athens. They made pottery from fine clay which was baked in an oven called a kiln until it became very hard.

These pots were used for carrying water and wine.

These pots were drinking cups.

The painter finished the pot.

Pots were baked in a kiln.

Most of the pots were made on a wheel. The apprentice turned the wheel for the potter.

First they shaped the wet clay on a wheel. Then they put the pots into the hot kiln to become dry and firm.

Red and black figure pottery

The Ancient Greeks liked to decorate their pots with drawings and paintings. These tell us a lot about how they lived.

Some potters made black figure pottery. They painted glaze onto the pots. This turned them black or dark brown when the pot was baked in the kiln. Lines were then scratched on the black glaze with a sharp tool to show the light clay beneath.

After many years, the Athenians invented a new way of making pottery. They painted the pots with black paint but left some parts red or orange. We call this red figure pottery.

These pots were used for mixing wine with water.

Different shapes for different uses

Greek pottery came in many shapes and sizes. Each pot or vase had its own special use. These are some of the many different shapes of pots and vases.

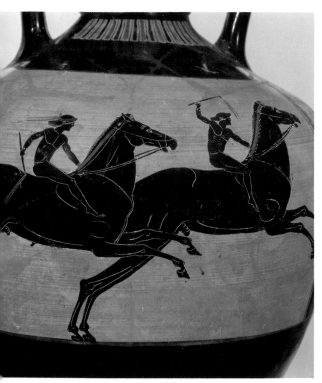

These pots were used to hold olive oil.

▲ This black figure pot shows horse racing in Ancient Greece.

▲ This red figure pot is decorated with a picture of Greek musicians.

The sculptor at work

In Ancient Greece there were many sculptors and artists who made beautiful objects out of marble, wood and metal. Some also made statues or objects out of baked clay, called terra cotta.

Most statues were carved out of marble. The sculptor used different kinds of tools to get the right shape.

Making statues from bronze

If sculptors wanted to make something from metal or terra cotta, they first had to make a mold. This is how sculpture was made from the metal we call bronze. Bronze is made by melting tin and copper and mixing them together.

▲ Greek terracotta figure.

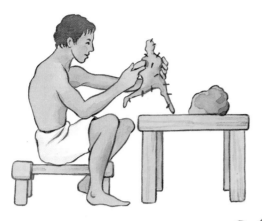

1. The sculptor makes the rough shape of the statue out of clay.

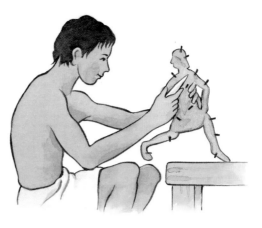

2. He covers the clay with wax and carves the fine detail.

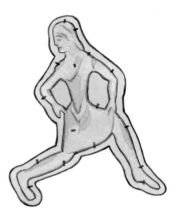

3. He then covers the carved wax statue with clay again. When he heats the whole statue, the clay becomes hard but the wax becomes soft and melts away.

4. He pours molten bronze into the space where the wax was.

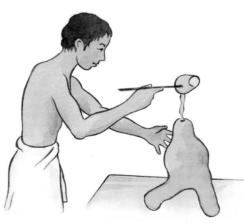

5. When the bronze cools it becomes hard. The clay on the outside is then removed.

◄ **Bronze statue of the Greek god Poseidon.**

The gods of Mount Olympus

In Greece there is a high mountain called Mount Olympus. For much of the year the top of the mountain is covered in cloud. The Ancient Greeks believed that this was the home of the gods and goddesses. They believed that the gods and goddesses looked down from the mountain on <u>mortal</u> men and women.

The gods were believed to sit round tables made of gold eating ambrosia and drinking nectar, which was a honey drink. Ambrosia helped them live forever.

ZEUS

King of the gods and god of the sky and the weather

▼ **Mount Olympus, home of the Ancient Greek gods and goddesses.**

GREEK GODS

HERA

Wife of Zeus and goddess of marriage and children

POSEIDON

God of the sea and earthquakes

ATHENE

Goddess of arts, wisdom and skill

APOLLO

God of the sun, light and music

ARTEMIS

Goddess of hunting and the moon

DIONYSUS

God of wine and the theater

HEPHAESTUS

God of fire and blacksmiths

ARES

God of war

APHRODITE

Goddess of love and beauty

HERMES

Messenger of the gods and god of travellers and thieves

DEMETER

Goddess of the crops

HADES

King of the underworld

31

Stories the Greeks told

1. Arachne was a woman who wove beautiful pictures. She thought she was as good at weaving as the goddess Athene.

Greek myths

The Greeks used to tell many stories about their gods and goddesses. We call these stories myths. This is the story of Athene and Arachne.

2. Athene disguised herself as an old woman and visited Arachne. She told her not to boast that she could weave better than Athene, but Arachne refused.

Greek legends

The Greeks also told many stories about heroes like Odysseus who sailed the Mediterranean Sea. We call these stories legends. The story of Odysseus was written in a long poem by a man called Homer. The poem is called "The Odyssey".

The picture on this vase tells the story of Odysseus and the Sirens. Odysseus and his sailors were warned about the Sirens by a woman called Circe. The Sirens were creatures that sang beautiful songs.

This is what Circe said to Odysseus;

Take your ship past the Sirens; but you must not let your men hear their singing or you will be drawn onto the rocks and your ship will be wrecked. Soften some wax and plug everyone's ears with this. If you want to hear the Sirens' beautiful song yourself, then make your crew tie you tightly to the mast with strong ropes.

3. Athene threw off her disguise and challenged Arachne to a weaving contest.

4. But Arachne wove just as well as the goddess.

5. Athene was so angry that she tore up Arachne's weaving.

6. Arachne tried to hang herself but was turned into a spider to hang forever on her thread.

The Underworld

The Greeks believed that when people died, their souls were taken by the god Hermes to the River Styx. Here they had to pay a ferryman called Charon to take them across the river to the Underworld. The Underworld was ruled by the god Hades.

In the Underworld, people who had led good lives were sent to a place called the Elysian fields where they would be forever happy. But people who had been wicked while they were alive were sent to a place called Tartarus to be punished.

In Tartarus each person was given a different punishment which lasted forever.

Tantalus tried to quench his terrible thirst but could never reach the water around him, or the grapes above his head.

The daughters of Danaus tried to fill pots which were full of holes.

Sisyphus tried to roll a huge stone uphill. As he got near the top, the stone rolled down again.

Tityus had his insides pecked by vultures.

Oracles and temples

Today, some people read their 'stars' in the newspaper to find out what will happen to them in the future. The Ancient Greeks believed that it was very important to find out about the future. Many travelled to Delphi to visit the temple or shrine of Apollo, god of <u>prophecy</u>. There they could ask the priestess of the temple to tell them about their future. This shrine was called the <u>Oracle</u>.

▶ **This is what the Priestess of Delphi may have looked like.**

▶ **The ruins of a temple at Delphi today.**

King Croesus and the Oracle

Herodotus tells of one famous visit to the Oracle at Delphi by a rich king called Croesus. Croesus was the ruler of an empire. He lived in a land called Lydia.

Croesus wanted to know if he should go to war with the Persians. The Oracle told him, "If Croesus attacks the Persians he will destroy a great empire."

I left the oracle feeling very happ and ordered my army to attack the Persians. But I should hav stopped to thin Can you gues why?

Why did the Greeks build temples?

We know that temples were very important to the Ancient Greeks. Temples were built to please the gods and goddesses so that they would be kind to the people that built them.

Outside the temples, people came to make sacrifices, by killing animals, to thank the gods for their good luck or to ask for help in the future. Sick people made sacrifices hoping the gods would cure them. If they did get better they would make sacrifices to say "thank you."

▲ This stone carving was given to the gods by someone to say 'thank you' for healing their leg.

Language and learning

The Ancient Greeks invented their own alphabet which helped them to put their ideas down in writing. Many of these writings still survive today.

There are many English words which come from Ancient Greek words. Here are some Greek words. What English words can you make from them?

Duo = 2

Treis = 3

Pente = 5

Hex = 6

Octo = 8

Deca = 10

Chronos = time

Polis = city

Techne = skill

Scopein = to look at

Peri = around

Dia = through

Cata = down

Polys = many

Micros = small

Megas = big

Teles = far off

Phone = voice

How many words can you find ending in the following Greek words?

−metry (measuring)
−logy (studying)
−graphy (writing about)

Great writers and thinkers

The Ancient Greeks used their alphabet to write history and poetry. They wrote plays that were performed in the theater. A great deal of what we know about the Greeks comes from their writings. Many books that were written in Ancient Greek have been translated into English and can be read today.

A Greek poet called Homer wrote two long poems called "The Iliad" and "The Odyssey." "The Iliad" is a poem about a great war that Greece fought against a city called Troy.

▲ Sculpture of a Greek called Sophocles who wrote many plays.

Some Ancient Greeks tried to explain the world around them, and suggest ways in which people may live good lives, and how they should be ruled. These great thinkers were called philosophers. Over 2,000 years later we still study their ideas.

▶ Sappho was a famous Greek writer. She also wrote poetry.

◀ Herodotus was a Greek writer who wrote about the past. He is known as the first real historian. He visited many lands including Egypt, and wrote about the pyramids, mummies, and the River Nile.

Science and mathematics

Many of the Ancient Greeks we remember today wrote books about science and mathematics, or made new discoveries or inventions.

A Greek scientist called Hero invented a way of using steam power. The machine he made was only a toy. He did not realize how useful his steam engine could have been!

▲ This Greek coin shows a famous Greek mathematician called Pythagoras.

Hero's steam engine.

How high are the Great Pyramids?

A Greek called Thales wanted to measure the height of the Great Egyptian Pyramids.

He noticed that all shadows change in length during the day. He put a stick in the ground and waited until its shadow was the same length as the stick.

At exactly the same time in the day he measured the shadow of the largest pyramid.

Greek doctors

Not all Greeks trusted the gods to cure them when they were ill. There were many doctors, the most famous of whom was Hippocrates.

▲ This stone carving shows a Greek doctor examining a child with stomach ache.

Sports and the Olympic Games

The Ancient Greeks liked to take part in sports. Sport kept them strong and fit and made them better fighters in times of war. Every four years the Olympic Games were held at the city of Olympia. They were also held in other places like Delphi where remains of a stadium have been found. We know that male athletes from all the Greek cities took part in the Olympics. Even in times of war people travelling to Olympia across enemy lands would not be harmed.

There were many different events at the games, including running, wrestling and boxing. The winners were given crowns made out of twigs cut from a sacred olive tree.

▼ **The stadium at Delphi today.**

The winning boxer was presented with an olive crown.

▲ The picture on this vase shows men taking part in a pentathlon. One is holding jumping weights used in the long jump. The others are holding the javelin and a discus.

Athletics was not only for men. We women had our own games at Olympia.

The theater

The Ancient Greeks held many special festivals when plays were put on in the theater. Most Ancient Greek cities had a theater and many can still be seen today. Plays were performed in the center and the audience sat on stone seats. The theaters were specially built so that every sound could be heard, even in the back row.

The main actors stood on a raised stage.

The circular area in front of the stage was called the orchestra. The actors who sang and danced here were called the chorus. In comedies they sometimes dressed as animals.

42

Tragedies and comedies

In the first plays people mostly sang songs and danced for the god of wine, Dionysus.

Later on, Athenian poets began to write plays for actors. The actors had their own words to speak and they wore special masks. Prizes were given for the best plays.

A tragedy was a play with a sad ending. A comedy was a play with lots of jokes to make the audience laugh.

◄ In large Greek theaters it was difficult for the audience to see the actors' faces. Masks helped them tell one actor from another. Can you tell which of these masks was for a comedy and which was for a tragedy?

imes actors
g gods were
p by a crane.

▼ The theater at Epidauros today.

43

Alexander
the Great

A famous Ancient Greek leader called
Alexander built a very strong army
trained in new ways of fighting. No
one could beat Alexander in battle. He
conquered all the lands of the old
Persian Empire, including Egypt. Many
Greeks went to settle in these lands.

Alexander was a great general who
used clever <u>tactics</u> to win battles. He
had a strong cavalry and foot-soldiers
armed with long spears.

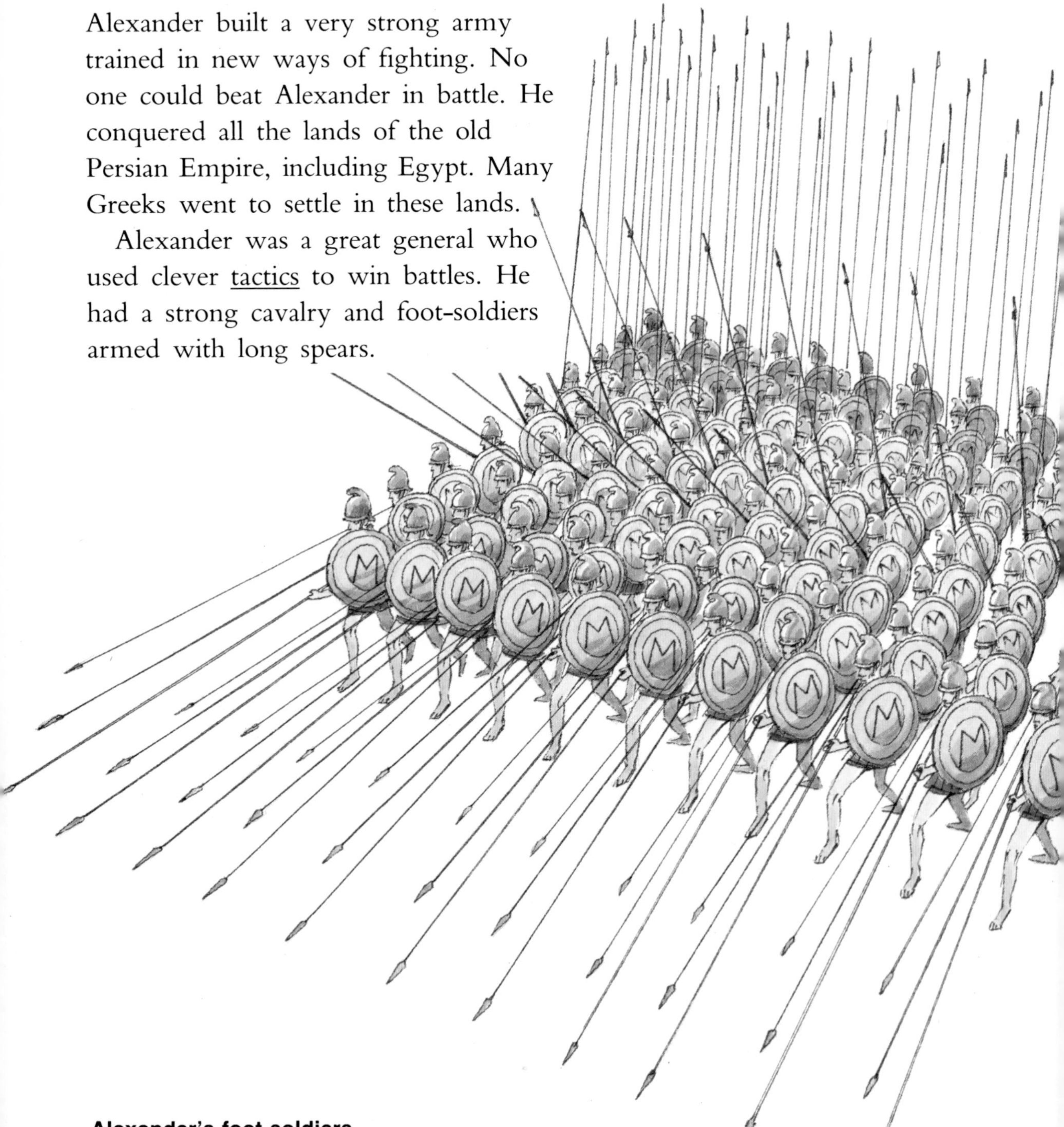

**Alexander's foot-soldiers
were difficult to attack when
they stood in a square.**

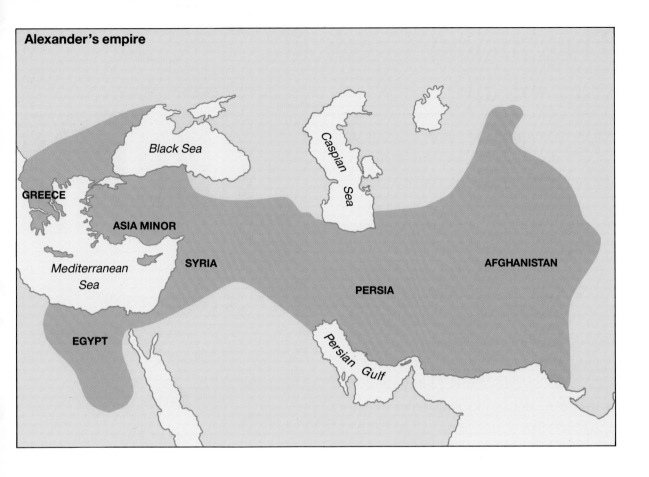

Alexander's empire

Black Sea

Caspian Sea

GREECE

ASIA MINOR

Mediterranean Sea

SYRIA

AFGHANISTAN

PERSIA

EGYPT

Persian Gulf

▼ This coin shows the head of Alexander the Great.

The city of Alexander

The Greeks built new cities in the lands Alexander had conquered. One city became very important. This was Alexandria, on the north coast of Egypt, named after Alexander. Traders sailed their ships to and from the city. A huge tower was built with a flame at the top to guide sailors into the harbor. This lighthouse was one of the wonders of the ancient world.

Many artists, writers and scientists lived and worked in Alexandria. A great library was built which contained many fine books. There may have been as many as half a million books!

The Ancient Greek way of life

After Alexander the Great had died, Greece was invaded by the Romans. Greece became part of the Roman Empire.

Large numbers of Greeks were taken prisoner to Rome where they became slaves. Most rich Romans wanted Greek slaves because they were well educated. They became the teachers of young Romans.

The Romans admired Greek art and ideas and copied them. They built Rome out of marble and decorated their temples with sculptures. They told stories of Greek gods and heroes and performed plays in open-air theaters. They decorated their pottery with people and made mosaic pictures out of hundreds of small stones. They wrote books about history, philosophy, science and medicine.

▲ **The Roman temple of Claudius in Colchester was built in the Greek style.**

Ancient Greece and the modern world

Even today we can see lots of things that remind us of the world of the Ancient Greeks.

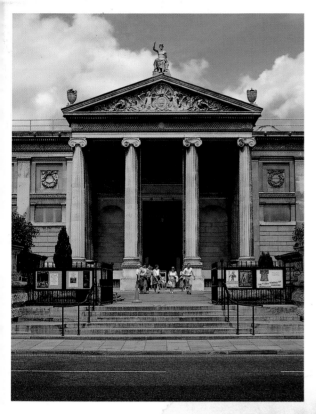

▲ **This museum in Oxford, England was built in the Greek style.**

Glossary

These words are underlined in this book.

Acropolis
The hill in Athens on which the Ancient Greeks built the Parthenon and other temples.

Archaeologists
People who have been trained to excavate (dig up) historical sites. They study the objects they find and tell us what life in the past may have been like.

Archers
Soldiers who fight using bow and arrows.

Empire
A large area of land and people ruled over by one king or emperor.

Festivals
Special days when people worshipped a particular god or goddess. They made sacrifices and held athletic events or plays in the honor of the god.

Hoplites
Heavily armed Greek soldiers who fought on foot.

Mortal
Living people who will die one day. The gods were immortal because they lived forever.

Olympic Games
The festival held in honor of Zeus at Olympia in southern Greece.

Oracle
A place where a god could be asked for advice about the future. Oracle also means the advice given by the god.

Parthenon
The great temple of Athene on the Acropolis in Athens.

Peloponnesian War
A long war (431–404 B.C.) fought between Athens and Sparta. Peloponnese is the name for the southern part of Greece.

Prophecy
Telling people about the future. Apollo was the god of prophecy.

Sacrifice
Offerings made by people to their god or goddess. Sometimes precious objects were offered or animals were burned in their honor.

Stadium
A special area where the Greeks held athletic contests and chariot races.

Tactics
Skillful plans made by an army in order to win a battle.